D1336673

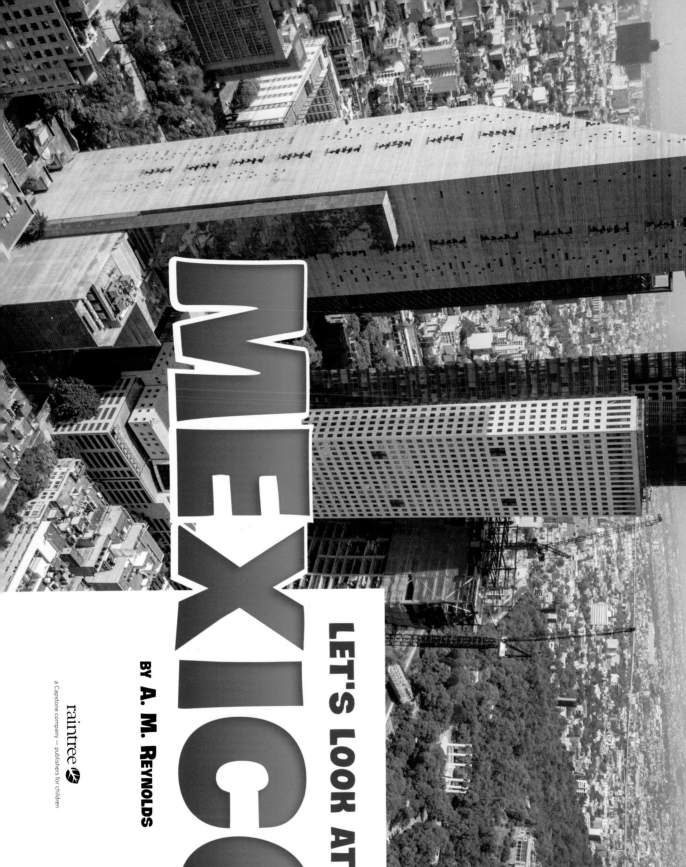

MEXICO

LET'S LOOK AT

BY A. M. REYNOLDS

raintree
a Capstone company — publishers for children

Pebble Plus

LET'S LOOK AT COUNTRIES

Raintree is an imprint of Capstone Global Library Limited, a company incorporated in England and Wales having its registered office at 264 Banbury Road, Oxford, OX2 7DY – Registered company number: 6695582

www.raintree.co.uk
myorders@raintree.co.uk

Text © Capstone Global Library Limited 2019
The moral rights of the proprietor have been asserted.

All rights reserved. No part of this publication may be reproduced in any form or by any means (including photocopying or storing it in any medium by electronic means and whether or not transiently or incidentally to some other use of this publication) without the written permission of the copyright owner, except in accordance with the provisions of the Copyright, Designs and Patents Act 1988 or under the terms of a licence issued by the Copyright Licensing Agency, Barnard's Inn, 86 Fetter Lane, London, EC4A 1EN (www.cla.co.uk). Applications for the copyright owner's written permission should be addressed to the publisher.

Edited by Erika L Shores
Designed by Juliette Peters
Picture research by Jo Miller
Production by Kathy McColley
Originated by Capstone Global Library Ltd
Printed and bound in India

ISBN 978 1 4747 6943 3
23 22 21 20 19
10 9 8 7 6 5 4 3 2 1

British Library Cataloguing in Publication Data
A full catalogue record for this book is available from the British Library.

Acknowledgements
We would like to thank the following for permission to reproduce photographs: Shutterstock: Aberu. Go, 1, Aleksandar Todorovic, 17, Anton_Ivanov, 9, 21, Art Konovalov, 19, Chepe Nicoli, Cover Top, EddieHernandezPhotography, 11, Globe Turner, 22 (Inset), IR Stone, Cover Middle, Jakub Zajic, 13, Kobby Dagan, 14, 15, nate, 4, Rafael Ramirez Lee, 22–23, 24, saad315, 8, Simon Dannhauer, 6, stacyarturogi, Cover Bottom, Cover Back, Sven Hansche, 3, THPStock, 7, Ulrike Stein, 5.

Every effort has been made to contact copyright holders of material reproduced in this book. Any omissions will be rectified in subsequent printings if notice is given to the publisher.
All the internet addresses (URLs) given in this book were valid at the time of going to press. However, due to the dynamic nature of the internet, some addresses may have changed, or sites may have changed or ceased to exist since publication. While the author and publisher regret any inconvenience this may cause readers, no responsibility for any such changes can be accepted by either the author or the publisher.

CONTENTS

Where is Mexico?

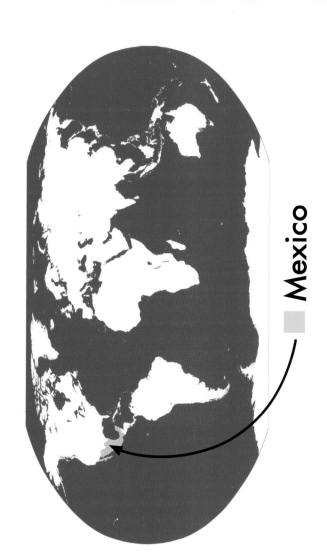

Mexico

Mexico is a country in North America. It is about eight times bigger than the UK. Mexico's capital is Mexico City.

Mexico City, Mexico

From rainforests to deserts

Mexico has mountains, rainforests, canyons and deserts. Three bodies of water surround Mexico.

It has many beaches.

ocelot

In the wild

Many types of animals live in Mexico.

Ocelots are wildcats that live

in rainforests. Howler monkeys swing

from treetops. Grey whales swim

in waters around Mexico.

howler monkey

People

Many Mexicans live in cities.

Most people live in the middle of the country.

Mexicans speak Spanish.

At the table

Traditional Mexican food has lots of herbs and vegetables. It is full of flavour.

Traditional foods include tacos, enchiladas and guacamole.

Festivals

Cities and towns hold fiestas

throughout the year.

These festivals have parades,

fireworks and mariachi bands

with guitars and trumpets.

At work

Many Mexicans work in shops and offices.

Some help tourists in hotels and restaurants.

Some people work in banks, hospitals

or schools.

Transport

Mexicans has many airports.

Only the United States and Brazil have more airports than Mexico.

In the countryside, many people travel by bus.

Famous place

Chichen Itza is an old city in Mexico.

The Mayan people built it

1,500 years ago. It has a 24-metre

(79-foot) tall pyramid.

QUICK MEXICO FACTS

Name: United Mexican States

Capital: Mexico City

Other major cities: Guadalajara, Puebla

Population: 124,574,795 (2017 estimate)

Size: 1,964,375 sq km (758,450 square miles)

Language: Spanish

Money: Mexican Peso

Mexican flag

GLOSSARY

fiesta holiday or festival in Mexico

guacamole mashed dip made from avocados

mariachi band small group of musicians who play lively music with trumpets and guitars

Mayan belonging to the ancient civilization of Maya

tourist someone who travels and visits other places for fun

traditional relating to ideas, ways and beliefs that are passed down from one generation to the next

FIND OUT MORE

BOOKS

Christmas in Mexico (Christmas Around the World),
Cheryl L. Enderlein (Raintree, 2017)

Mexico (A Benjamin Blog and His Inquisitive Dog Guide),
Anita Ganeri (Raintree, 2014)

Recipes from Mexico (Cooking Around the World),
Dana Meachen Rau (Raintree, 2015)

WEBSITES

www.bbc.com/bitesize/articles/zqv6msg
Learn more about the Mayans.

www.dkfindout.com/uk/earth/continents/north-america
Find out more about North America.

COMPREHENSION QUESTIONS

1. What language is spoken in Mexico?

2. Name two things you might see at a fiesta.

3. What transport is used by many people in the countryside?

INDEX